How to Make A

ZERO
BACKWARDS

An Activity Book for the Imagination

by Richard Kehl

SCHOLASTIC

New York   Toronto   London   Auckland   Sydney

To Shau Shum

ISBN 0-590-42547-1

Copyright © 1989 by Richard Kehl.

12 11 10 9 8 7 6 5 4 3 2 1   9/8 0 1 2 3/9

Printed in the U.S.A.   08

First Scholastic printing, November 1989

INTRODUCTION

How To Make a Zero Backwards is an idea of one way you can do something really differently. That's what this book is all about—doing ordinary things in wonderful new ways. Each project will encourage you to see things freshly, as if for the first time.

I have shared these activities with thousands of young people and have discovered that everyone is able to come up with creative and original ideas.

Have fun with all the projects. Let your imagination go free. You may be amazed at what you can create!

Richard Kehl

A Book

ake twenty-seven pieces of paper and tie or staple them together on one side, or use a ring notebook. Write your name and *ABC Book* on the outside of the first page. For example, *Richard Kehl's ABC Book*.

Starting with the letter *A*, each of the pages in your book will illustrate a different letter of the alphabet. Look through magazines for pictures you can use for each letter. Take as much time as you like; think of this as a collection.

When you have as many pictures as you need for a letter, paste them down in an interesting design. Include the letter you are illustrating somewhere in the design.

Go from *A* to *Z*, and you will have a book!

HINT: Your book would make a fine gift for a friend or relative. You can photocopy what you have done and become a published author.

THINGS IN THE MAIL

It is amazing what will get through the mail, if it is done with a spirit of good will and humor.

Here are some things I have mailed without any problem:

individual pieces of a jigsaw puzzle

a transparent glove stuffed with candy

a wooden fish holding the address in his mouth

a Hershey bar

a cloth doll

a phonograph record (without its sleeve)

a broken boomerang in a clear plastic envelope

Your challenge is to think of things to mail to your friends or relatives that will delight them. Be sure nothing you send has sharp edges that might harm postal workers.

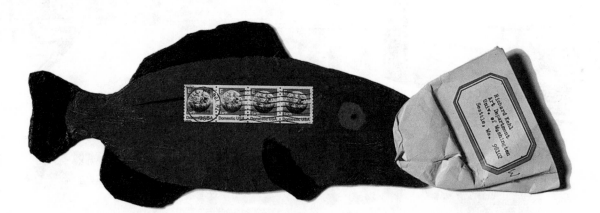

HINT: Put twice as much postage on each item as weight requires. Mark "HAND CANCEL."

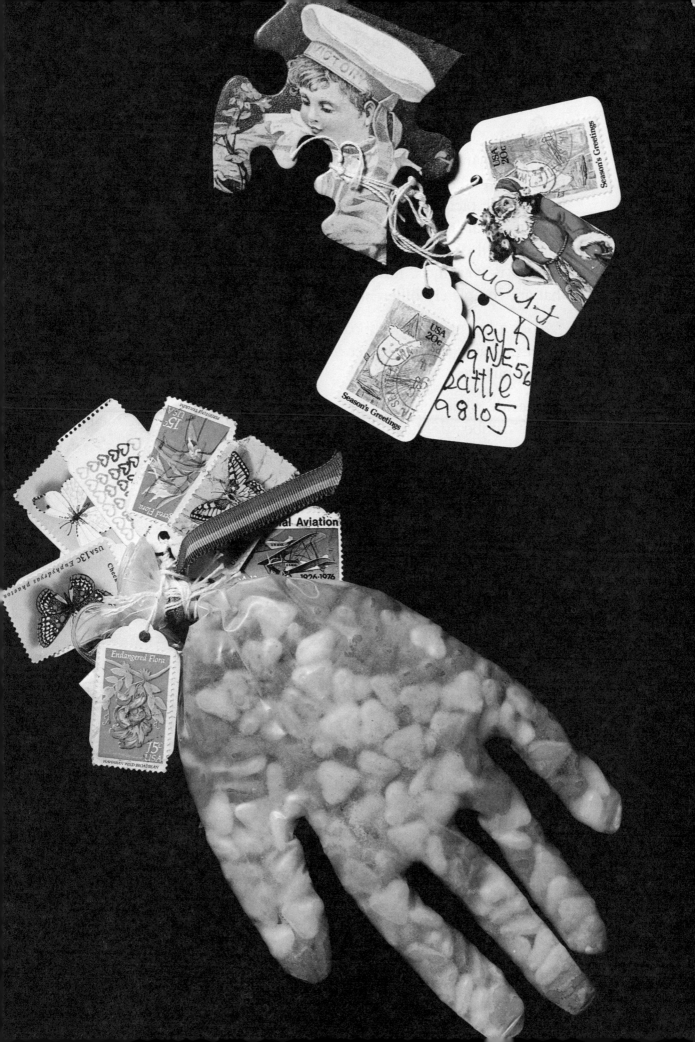

CARNIVAL FRONT

At many carnivals and street fairs you can get your photograph taken with your face sticking through a hole in a lifesize picture of a famous person. Now make your own "carnival front." A skeleton, a robot, a clown, a large animal — all of these would be excellent choices for your front. It is even more fun if you make two or more figures that are completely different.

Get a big piece of cardboard (the bigger the better). You'll probably be able to get one free at a store that sells appliances.

Decide what figure (or figures) you want, then paint it on the cardboard. Make sure the figure is as big as you are, or bigger. You can paint the rest of the cardboard a solid color, or make a scene around the figure.

Cut a tall, oval hole eight inches tall and six inches wide in the face of each figure.

Hang or stand your cardboard painting so that people can stand behind it and place their faces in the holes.

Take photographs of you and your friends.

HINT: Copies of these photographs make excellent gifts for friends and relatives.

TRADING CARDS

It is easy to make your own trading cards to swap with friends. Choose a favorite subject. Collect pictures of your subject from magazines or newspapers. Mount your pictures on heavy paper, and cut them to a uniform size. Some suggestions for card collections are:

comic book heroes   things that can fly   cars

people smiling   movie stars   butterflies

mammals   things of one color   musical performers

round things   dinosaurs   birds

airplanes   flowers

HINT: Encourage your friends to create their own cards, and then start a trading network. You can copy your cards and trade copies.

FLOWERS FROM THEIR NAMES

These are the names of real flowers and plants. Choose several that appeal to you. Make sure you don't know what they really look like. Think about each name until a picture comes into your mind. Now make that picture.

feather bush	milkweed	candytuft
wall flower	pigweed	blue cup flower
weeping willow	butterfly bush	mouse-ear
ice plant	cat's foot	fireweed
moonflower	pitcher plant	pepper-and-salt
cloud grass	ironweed	shooting star
baby's breath	rocket snapdragon	bearberry
rainbow rock grass	trumpet vine	sunflower
morning glory	foxglove	ghostflower
zebra bush	ladyslipper	unicorn plant

Zebra bush

HINT: You can either draw what you imagine, or you can look for pictures that you can cut out and combine.

Cerefa dulcia

MIXED-UP ANIMALS

Collect many pictures of animals from magazines. Cut each of them into three pieces — the head, main body, and rear end. Put all the heads in one pile, the bodies in a second, and rear ends in a third pile. Now make new creatures by mixing up the parts in interesting ways.

Don't forget to include men, women, and children in the assortment of animals.

HINT: You can make this an even more exciting experiment. Instead of dividing each animal into three parts, cut them into many more. Make piles of legs, arms, ears, noses, hands, etc.

SKY, HANDLE, SHOE

ake a painting, collage, or three dimensional object that includes sky, a handle, and a shoe. It is a strange combination, but it encourages fresh thinking.

For example, draw a window with a sky. The window has a handle on it. Outside a bird wearing shoes is flying by.

Add a handle to the back of an old shoe. Paint a sky with stars on the tongue.

Decorate a tray (with handles) to look like the sky. Put baby shoes or horseshoes on the tray.

HINT: Almost anything can use a handle.

An Eye Chart

Optometrists use charts with different-size letters and numbers to test people's eyesight. These charts, aside from their usefulness, are very attractive with their arrangement of big to small.

Make your own eye chart, using pictures instead of letters and numbers.

What you need is a single idea for your chart. Instead of letters you could use:

sources of light (suns to fireflies)

mammals (whale to mouse)

homes (castles to birds' nests)

flowers (sunflower to violet)

dogs (Great Dane to Pekinese)

musical instruments (grand piano to piccolo)

fruits (watermelon to grapes)

circus stars (elephant to trained flea)

timekeepers (Big Ben to wristwatch)

birds (eagle to hummingbird)

HINT: This exercise will be more enjoyable if you think of your own ideas. Use this list to inspire your thinking.

LETTER CHART FOR 20 FEET
Snellen Scale

20/40

20/20

PICTURE MAGNETS

uy magnetic strips at a hardware store. These are like thick tape. One side has a gummed surface covered with paper, and the other side will grip steel.

Now cut out some favorite pictures from magazines. Glue these pictures to heavy paper, and then cut out the figures with scissors. Put a small piece of your magnetic tape on the back of each picture. Your picture will now stick to a refrigerator door or other metallic surfaces.

Some suggestions for picture magnets:

comic strip characters
movie stars
animals
sports heroes
food
automobiles

trees
family members
flowers
everyday objects like telephones, pencils, television sets, etc.

Cat magnets

HINT: Experiment with arranging your picture magnets on your refrigerator door.

MAGIC NAMES

Below are the names of tricks that magicians perform. The names are almost as imaginative as the tricks themselves.

Pick out the name of a trick you like. Take some time to think about it. Now make a picture that illustrates the name, using cut-outs from magazines or newspapers, or create your own drawing or painting.

Living Photographs

The Flying Lamp

The Liquid Knife

Removing a Man's Shirt Without Removing His Coat

The Laughing Mirror

Paper that Tears Itself

The Smoking Rose

Sketching with Fire

Catching Fish in Midair

The Hypnotized Teaspoons

The Enchanted Hat

Obedient and Disobedient Eggs

Electric Shadows

Dance of the Bubbles

Climbing Through a Playing Card

The Knowing Arrow

Climbing Through a Playing Card

HINT: Don't try to make your ideas or pictures sensible. This project is meant to encourage creative thinking.

Catching Fish in Midair

A Visit to a Strange Land

Imagine you are about to go on a journey to a strange land where no one knows your language.

Before you go, prepare yourself with a set of homemade cards made of pictures that will help you communicate. Think of the wordless signs you see every day—road signs and signs in public places. (Some are shown below.) Find pictures that convey simple concepts, paste them on pieces of cardboard, and you will be ready for strange lands and new people.

HINT: Collect your cards in a small box. Carry them with you and try to communicate with your friends without using words.

The pictures on the next page tell a story.
Can you figure it out?
Turn the page upside down and see if you were right.

The story tells how someone (you?) got up one morning, got dressed, fed your cat, and ate breakfast. You brushed your teeth and then set off on a trip in an airplane. You flew to an exotic island where you saw exotic flowers and friendly animals. Night came and you saw other animals—scary ones. Then you found some tools and cloth and built a sailboat. You sailed home again.

BASIC IDEAS

his is a list of some of the basic ways in which things stand in relation to one another.

top	between	other
through	separated	alike
next to	behind	around
inside	in order	always
some (not many)	center	whole
never	away from	left
below	beginning	different

Pick out one, and then make a picture that illustrates it. This may not be easy at first, but it is an excellent exercise for the mind.

Through

HINT: You can make a game of this, like charades. Give each player a copy of this list. Each in turn acts out one of the concepts silently, and the player who guesses the correct idea wins.

Between

SELF-PORTRAIT

et a large photograph of yourself. If you don't have one that can be played with, make a photocopy of a photo.

Go through a pile of old magazines, and cut out pictures of little things that you like.

Now take the picture of yourself and add to it the little pictures that you collected. You should try to show things about yourself that are not usually visible. For example, a boy who loves baseball could put a ball and bat on his forehead. A girl who enjoys movies could place a little photo of a reel of film or a movie theater marquee over her heart.

HINT: Do the same thing with pictures of your friends, family, or pets.

SKY SHOP

ou are going to create a little shop or stand where things that go into the sky are sold. The challenge is to find and make as many things as possible.

Some possibilities:

parachutes	kites	fireflies
birds	flying fish	clouds
soap bubbles	moons (crescent, half, and full)	frisbees
rainbows		Cupid
airplanes	moonbeams	stars
dirigibles	snowflakes	fireworks
Peter Pan	sky repair kit	Pegasus, the winged horse
comets	balloons	
	flying elephant	

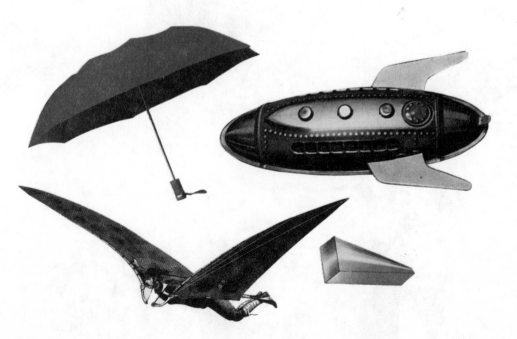

HINT: The shop (which can be as simple as a table) can be decorated suitably with a backdrop painted half as a black night sky, and half as a pale blue daytime sky. Objects from the shop can be displayed on this backdrop.

BOTTOM AND TOP

Ask a friend to pick out a large picture from a magazine, and then cut it in half (cutting from side to side). You must not look at the picture before it is cut. Your friend saves the top half and gives you the bottom half.

Now you glue this piece of the picture at the bottom of a sheet of paper. On the top you draw and paint, finishing the picture.

After you have finished, look at the top half that your friend saved. A comparison of your version with the original should be interesting.

HINT: Choose a picture of a single, tall object that fills the page, such as a giraffe, a tall candlestick, a skyscraper, a close-up of an ice cream cone, etc. Pictures that have many objects in them are not good for this project.